Lake District Villages

PHOTOGRAPHS BY
Val Corbett

MYRIAD
LONDON

GW00717057

AMBLESIDE

Surrounded by beautiful mountain scenery, Ambleside lies on the main road that runs between Keswick and Kendal. It is much more than a village – it even has its own cinema. Ambleside has a thriving student community at St Martin's College and hosts the Lake District Summer Music Festival

Ambleside is always busy. Although the centre bustles with shops and traffic, the oldest part, just off the road called "The Struggle" – the route up to the Kirkstone Pass – has some lovely old houses and streets to explore. Peggy Hill, off North Road, and sharply uphill from Stock Bridge, is a good place to start.

Bridge House, the unusual National Trust property, straddles Stock Beck and beyond it, the old mill buildings, complete with water-wheel, are now a restaurant. Further up Stock Ghyll are former corn and bobbin mills and higher still there are attractive waterfalls.

Waterhead (below) is an outlying part of Ambleside and is a busy centre for boating at the northern point of Windermere. Nearby Borrans Park is a tranquil place overlooking the lake with the remains of the important Roman fort, Galava, still visible nearby.

Below: the oldest and quaintest part of Ambleside close to Stock Bridge is well worth exploring on foot. St Mary's *(left and above)* has a 180ft (55m) spire which makes it an easily recognisable landmark all over town. The church was built by George Gilbert Scott and completed in 1854

ASKHAM *left & far left*

Described by the famous fell-walker and writer Alfred Wainwright as the most attractive village in Westmorland, Askham lies five miles south of Penrith on the road to Haweswater

Askham boasts an exceptionally long and wide green bounded by pretty white cottages and houses, several of which have date stones from the 17th century. The best approach is from Lowther Park, crossing the old bridge over the River Lowther and then climbing sharply uphill by the church. The two pleasant pubs are popular and the village shop is at the centre of the village in every sense. A popular summer attraction is the open-air heated swimming pool.

Askham Hall is a mainly Tudor addition to an earlier pele tower and is the present family home of Lord Lonsdale. Heughscar Hill is a gentle uphill walk from the village. It is an area rich in prehistoric remains and offers spectacular views over Ullswater.

Right: many of the older houses in Askham, built in the 17th century, display the dates of their construction above the front door

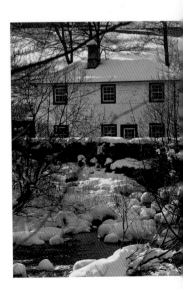

BASSENTHWAITE *below*

Most of this village is down a narrow side road off the A591, six miles north of Keswick. Access to quiet mountain scenery is particularly good

Bassenthwaite is well away from the busy tourist centres, and apart from some tourist accommodation, it gives the impression of being an ordinary village without the normal commercial features of a holiday area. There are even working farms in the village centre. This quiet unspoiled charm also extends to the neighbouring villages of Ireby and Uldale.

Dash Beck rises "back o' Skiddaw" and cascades over Whitewater Dash then, two miles downstream, flows past a pretty grassy area and playground in the village. St John's Church lies close to the main road but another parish church, the ancient church of St Bega, is set in a prominent position near the lake shore just north of Mirehouse.

During the Scarecrow Festival, dozens of scarecrows seem to take over the village and locals compete to come up with the most original design.

Once a separate village, Bowness is now joined to the town of Windermere. It is a bustling lakeside spot and a magnet for tourists arriving from the south

Bowness is one of the tourist hotspots of the Lake District but nonetheless retains much charm with corners of the original quaint settlement intact and the stylish Victorian mansions built by the newly-wealthy from Lancashire still surviving as hotels. Despite some ill-conceived planning blunders, the lake front is enjoyable with its traditional ticket offices, flower beds, ducks and swans. Above all it presents the visitor with an endless display of boats manoeuvring in and out of the bay or just the chance to watch other people enjoy themselves.

A peaceful contrast is offered by a short walk south to Cockshott Point with its close views of Belle Isle and its unusual circular, domed mansion.

Left: Blackwell, one of Britain's most important Arts & Crafts houses, occupies a stunning position overlooking Windermere, one mile south of Bowness. The house is open to the public.
Below: the landing stage at Bowness

BOOT *right*

The last settlement up the Eskdale Valley, Boot lies three miles west of Hardknott, the most challenging road pass in the Lake District

The parish church of Boot, the 12th century St Catherine's, is a little distance from the village across fields, with a lovely setting on the River Esk where stepping stones cross to the further bank.

Iron-mining in the 19th century significantly enlarged the then small

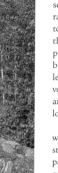

settlement of Boot. The three-foot gauge railway, known as "La'al Ratty", was built to transport the ore seven miles down to the railway at Ravenglass. However, the price of iron collapsed and the mining business proved shortlived. After a lengthy period of disuse, enthusiastic volunteers renovated the scenic little line and it soon developed into the much-loved attraction it is today.

Eskdale Mill, the old village corn mill which dates from the 16th century (left), stands on the far side of the picturesque packhorse bridge over Whillan Beck. It is one of the few remaining water-driven corn mills in Britain and can usually be seen in operation. Close to the mill pond there is a glorious picnic spot.

BRAITHWAITE *above & right*

The busy A66 skirts Braithwaite, which is tucked away at the foot of the Whinlatter Pass two miles west of Keswick. It is a common starting point for the strenuous nine-mile Coledale round mountain walk

Braithwaite has a great number of hidden attractions and a walk around the footpaths and little roads reveals some eye-catching corners. The higher parts of the village enjoy fine views of the Skiddaw massif.

The Coledale Beck adds greatly to the charm of the village and can be crossed and re-crossed on the various bridges. Very shortly upstream, there is a good place to picnic and paddle in the pool created by the weir. The village shop looks useful for either locals or visitors.

A miners' track leads to the head of Coledale, where mining for barytes and zinc took place until recently at Force Crag Mine. The mining buildings are still clearly visible along with the waste soil dug out of the ground.

BROUGHTON IN FURNESS *below*

One of the most attractive large villages in the Lake District, Broughton is on the southern tip of the national park, seven miles from Coniston Lake. The village manages successfully to tread the fine line of catering well for visitors, yet at the same time remaining a village with a local feel

The handsome square is dominated by chestnut trees, which are a lovely sight in May with their flowering "candles". In the centre of the square is a pair of stocks, an obelisk and some old stone slabs. On the south side, the 17th-century town hall with its seven arches, clock and weather vane, make an architecturally interesting home for the tourist information centre.

Broughton Mills with its picturesque pub (above) is a tiny hamlet in an idyllic valley two miles north of Broughton. The tiny but picturesque Holy Innocents Church is well worth a visit.

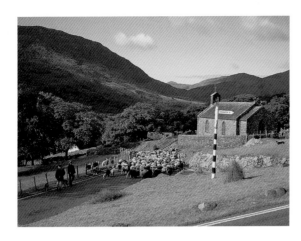

BUTTERMERE *above & below*

Buttermere can be reached either from the Newlands or Honister passes. The village lies close to low-lying water meadows where cows were kept, giving Buttermere its name. Crummock Water is just across the fields

The beautifully-sited church of St James is perched on a rocky knoll above Buttermere village and has views of the lake and the surrounding high fells. A simple carved stone memorial to Alfred Wainwright, the famous fell-walker and writer, is in one of the church window-sills and there is a view from the window across to Haystacks, his favourite mountain where his ashes are scattered. The porch has a functional yet decorative iron gate showing a shepherd with his sheep.

Buttermere village itself consists of little more than a farm and two hotels, the Bridge and the Fish. The latter became famous for being the home of Mary Robinson who was called "The Beauty of Buttermere". Tourists would travel to the inn just to catch sight of her. However she was duped into a bigamous marriage by a scoundrel. An attractive spot just close to the Bridge Hotel is Mill Beck which flows in a torrent just under a bridge on its way to Crummock Water.

From Buttermere you can climb up Scale Pike or walk along the footpath to Scale Force, the highest waterfall in the Lake District.

CARTMEL *above, below & right*

Cartmel lies on one of the limestone peninsulas on the southern edge of the Lake District that reach into the flat expanse of Morecambe Bay. This extremely picturesque village is two miles west of Grange-Over-Sands and is best known for its ancient priory

Cartmel Priory, founded in 1188, towers over the village. Although much of it was destroyed in the Dissolution, the priory church and the gatehouse in the village square still survive. The interior of the church is vast but rich in fascinating detail. The Eea (which means river!) flows

Top: Cartmel Priory
Above and left: Cartmel Village Shop on the village square, home of sticky toffee pudding. Outside of the six or so steeplechase meetings each year at the local racecourse, Cartmel is a sleepy and picturesque retreat

through the village, adding charm to the side streets with their handsome houses. The two pubs are both welcoming and the range of little shops includes The Cartmel Village Shop which stocks a wide range of Cumbrian foods. The owners also make the original diet-defying but almost irresistible sticky toffee pudding, which they sell throughout Britain. On the far edge of the village, Cartmel racecourse has regular steeplechase meetings during the summer and makes a useful car park at other times.

CALDBECK right

This attractive village is packed with historical evidence of its busy industrial and mining past. It lies on the quiet far northern edge of the national park, 14 miles south of Carlisle

Caldbeck is well-known for being the home of John Peel, the famous Cumbrian huntsman. His ornate gravestone in the churchyard of St Kentigern draws visitors to the village but Caldbeck has a great deal more to offer. The Cald Beck – "the cold stream" – flows behind the church and close to the old bridge there is an interesting well. There is a pleasant walk downstream to Priests Mill, a converted watermill with craft shops and a good café.

Upstream is The Howk, containing a large ruined bobbin mill (below), dramatic gorge and waterfalls. Though now peaceful and with a much reduced population, the village was booming for centuries with many mills and mining in the nearby fells.

CHAPEL STILE right

The road from Ambleside to Coniston branches at Skelwith Bridge. Take the right-hand fork to Great Langdale past Elterwater and you reach Chapel Stile. As you approach the village, it seems that with each turn in the road, the scenery becomes wilder and more dramatic

Chapel Stile is the type of place where it feels perfectly normal to meet sheep walking along the middle of the village street or grazing on the verge.

The sturdy church, with its fortified tower, serves the whole of Langdale and is a fine sight rising above the village with Silver Howe as a backdrop. The Cumbria Way long-distance footpath enjoys this same view as it passes the village.

Slate quarrying, both past and present, is evident everywhere; the scree on the fellside, the occasional boom of quarry blasting and the village houses themselves which are almost all built from slate.

The independent Chapel Stile Co-op situated on the main road is a useful shopping stop, with a café upstairs that remains open all year. The local pub, the Wainwright's Inn, is welcoming with its open fires and stone-flagged floors.

CROSTHWAITE *left*

This little village lies in the Lyth Valley at the heart of the damson-growing area on the Kendal to Winster road

In late April the Lyth and Winster valleys are a wonderful sight with the profusion of white damson blossom in the little orchards which abound in the area. The sheltered and warmer climate of southern Lakeland is ideal for growing damsons, and in recent years the decline in some of the old orchards has been reversed as they have been restored to their earlier glory.

Each spring, the Westmorland Damson Association holds a Damson Day at Howe, near Crosthwaite, to promote awareness of the fruit. Guided walks, passing lovely old farms and orchards are among the highlights. The fruit is made into a huge variety of products including damson gin, damson beer, damson chocolates and, of course, the best of all – damson jam. Crosthwaite is just one of the villages in the damson-producing area, but its village shop (and that of Bowland Bridge) is a good place to buy damson products, as well as its own damson chutney and damson gumbo.

CONISTON *above & right*

The approach to Coniston from the south is on perhaps the worst A-road in England! The village lies between Coniston Old Man and the lake, and its history owes a lot to slate quarrying and copper mining in the hills behind

The Ruskin museum in the village is strong on the mining history of the area and also commemorates both John Ruskin and Donald Campbell, names that immediately spring to mind when Coniston is mentioned. Campbell's jet-powered *Bluebird* catastrophically back-flipped at high speed and sank here in 1967 during an attempt on the water speed record. Ruskin – artist, writer, critic, philosopher and social campaigner – spent his last 30 years at Brantwood on the opposite shore of the lake. He transformed the house into a beautiful home and it is now open to the public displaying his works and collections.

Two boats ply from the end of Lake Road to Brantwood, one of them being the restored steam yacht, *Gondola* (left), which is owned by the National Trust.

The microbrewery at the Black Bull is notable for its "Bluebird bitter", a winner of the Campaign for Real Ale's Supreme Champion Beer of Britain.

DACRE *left & right*

This small village of pretty cottages with its ancient moated castle, fascinating church and good pub lies on a minor road leading from the A66 to Ullswater, six miles south-west of Penrith

The Norman church of St Andrew's (right) is beautifully cared for by its proud parishioners. A large stone bear marks each corner of the churchyard but the origin of the bears is mysterious and their significance a puzzle. Inside the church there are many monuments to the Hassell family of Dalemain, including a superb modern window. Another modern window commemorates Willie Whitelaw, the Conservative politician who is buried at the church. On the floor is an engraved stone, thought to be a Viking grave.

The stately home of Dalemain, with its famous garden, is one mile as the crow flies from Dacre. The path follows an easy track through farmland to the river. It first passes Dacre Castle, originally one of the 14th-century pele towers built to defend the English border against the Scottish reivers.

ELTERWATER *right*

This much-visited little village, four miles west of Ambleside, is set in a popular Lake District valley. Its pretty little slate cottages were formerly used to house quarrymen but now many are used for holiday accommodation

Elterwater is scenically placed at the entrance to the Langdale valley and shares its name with the adjacent small lake. The first view of the village, coming either from Grasmere or Ambleside, is always impressive with the Coniston Fells and Langdale Pikes forming a dramatic background.

Although only tiny, the village has a characterful and popular pub (above), a good shop and an interesting handful of galleries. It was formerly industrial, with the houses being built for the workers at the adjacent green slate quarries. There was also a gunpowder factory, which is now the site of a timeshare complex. A walking route to Little Langdale takes in views of old and new slate quarries.

Elterwater is the smallest of the 16 Lake District lakes. "Elter" is the Norse word for "swan" so Elterwater literally means "Swan Lake".

GLENRIDDING *above*

The largest village on Ullswater, Glenridding lies near the southern end of the lake on the Kirkstone Pass road. Glenridding is a natural setting-off point for boat trips and mountain exploration

On fair weather weekends, crowds of walkers leave Glenridding, causing something approaching rush-hour conditions as they set off for Striding Edge. For the less ambitious, the Ullswater steamers (right) will ferry you throughout the year to Howtown or Pooley Bridge. This and the bus service provide opportunities for many linear walks.

The village owes its existence to the very successful lead-mining at Greenside. The mine made history by being the first to instal electricity, generated from water from Keppel Cove under Helvellyn.

With a plentiful choice of accommodation and an excellent tourist information centre, the village is a good base for visitors.

Legend has it that Patrick, the patron saint of Ireland, preached here and carried out baptisms. A holy well dedicated to the saint can be found close to the roadside just a mile south of the village.

GRANGE IN BORROWDALE *above & below*

Grange is near the southern end of Derwent Water, four miles from Keswick and accessible by roads on either side of the lake. A short distance upstream, the "Jaws of Borrowdale" leave just enough room for the road and river to snake through

The low-slung twin arches of Grange Bridge span the two branches of the river Derwent that flow either side of a small island, a popular spot for children to play on a summer day. Most buildings hereabouts are constructed from green slate and the slate pebbles and stones that line the riverbed give the clear water a striking blue-green translucence.

The good bus service gives opportunities for linear walks further into the Borrowdale valley, many following sections of the Cumbria Way. Nearby is a short and, in places, steep walk to Castle Crag but well worth the effort for the view from its summit.

The interior of Holy Trinity Church is unexpected with a barrel-shaped ceiling supported by beams aggressively finished with an unusual saw-toothed design.

GRASMERE *below & right*

Grasmere is in the very heart of the Lake District, just off the main road from Ambleside to Keswick. It is at the centre of some of Lakeland's most beautiful landscapes and has strong literary connections

Dove Cottage (right) was the home of William Wordsworth for the most creative period of his life. The day-to-day life of the poet, his family and their many visitors is brilliantly described by his sister Dorothy in her diaries. The cottage with its tiny rooms is still much as it would have been when the Wordsworths lived there. Throughout the day, enthusiastic guides lead well-informed and lively tours and the adjacent museum extends the experience. An impressive modern building houses an extensive collection of early and original material from the Lakes' poets.

Grasmere is also home to the famous Grasmere gingerbread, which is more like a deliciously spicy shortbread than cake, and is sold from the tiny cottage on the edge of the churchyard of St Oswald's.

HARTSOP *left*

Hartsop is situated in a sheltered side-valley near Brothers Water at the northern foot of Kirkstone Pass

Visitors generally arrive on foot at this quiet, unspoiled village. In the past it was busy with mining, quarrying and milling. It is worth a short walk along the track to the Hayeswater reservoir to see the impressive ruins of the watercourse and wheel pit of the former Mires Head lead mine. On the return path to the left are the remains of a corn mill with its grinding stones.

Although there are "spinning galleries" in the village, these were probably used as passages in the houses and for the display of fleeces rather than for spinning.

About a mile to the south-east and across Brothers Water lies a picturesque farm, Hartsop Hall, which was originally built in the 16th century. In the past, Brothers Water was called Broad Water, but was re-named after the tragic drowning of two brothers in the 19th century.

The Kirkstone Pass (1489ft/454m) is the highest road pass in the Lake District. It provides wonderful views over the surrounding fells and Brothers Water.

HESKET NEWMARKET *left*

Hesket Newmarket is a village in the far north of the Lake District, which lies close to its larger neighbour, Caldbeck. It is home to a unique brewery and pub

Beers brewed at the Old Crown Inn, the Hesket Newmarket pub, are nearly all named after Lake District fells, one exception being Doris's 90th Birthday Ale, dedicated to the mother-in-law of the founder. Shares in both the pub and the brewery were sold mainly to local people, enabling the two cooperatives to be set up and a unique partnership now exists. The initiative is particularly heartening at a time when some other village pubs are giving up.

The village is beautiful, with traditional houses ranged around a wide village green. A useful village shop doubles as a tea shop, closed only on Sunday.

A footpath leaves the green opposite the pub and leads to Watersmeet, the junction of Cald Beck and the River Caldew. Bluebells carpet the wooded banks in early summer.

A log book in the pub records details of the "Old Crown Round" in which walkers or runners must traverse the summits of Skiddaw, Blencathra, Carrock Fell and Great Cockup in a maximum time of 20 hours starting and finishing at the pub.

HAWKSHEAD *right & below*

Roughly midway between Windermere and the northern end of Coniston Water, this famous village lies just north of Esthwaite Water and near Tarn Hows. It is a compact maze of highly picturesque whitewashed buildings

Although chock-a-block with visitors and tourist shops, the restriction of cars into the village makes exploration here more enjoyable. The streets include squares, archways and alleys overhung in traditional 17th-century style.

Hawkshead is closely linked to Wordsworth's early life. His desk at the grammar school is on view there in what is now a museum. "Grammar school" does not have today's meaning and it is hard to imagine how 100 pupils could have been accommodated. Wordsworth lodged in Anne Tyson's cottage (below), half a mile away at Colthouse. Anne is reputed to have had a great influence on him: she was a gifted storyteller and may have sparked an interest in tales of the countryside in the young poet.

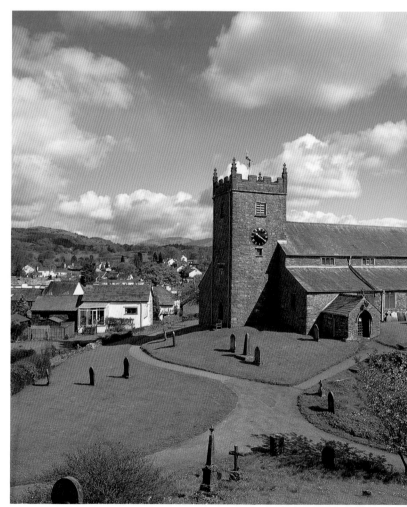

Right and above right: the appealing church of St Michael's and All Angels dominates the village from its position high on Hawkshead Hill and gives fine views to Esthwaite Water, Latterbarrow and Helvellyn.

The church contains a series of painted murals dating from 1680. Hawkshead developed rapidly in the Middle Ages thanks to the local wool trade. The town acted as a market for local wool which was then taken by boat to Kendal to be woven into the famous Kendal green cloth

KENTMERE *right*

Kentmere, in a quiet valley of the same name, is a village of scattered settlements and beautiful farmhouses near the end of the narrow and winding road from Staveley

Chickens scratch around in the fields above Kentmere Hall, a 15th-century manor house built on to an earlier defensive pele tower. The derivation of the name "Kentmere" appears strange as there is no lake, apart from the reservoir at the head of the valley. However, below the village, an area that originally was a lake was drained to provide water for the mills at nearby Staveley, leaving only a narrow strip of water.

Parking in the village is extremely limited, but the Kentmere Rover bus service is useful in summer. Because of the nature of the roads (Kentmere is built at the end of a narrow dead-end road) the valley is best not viewed from behind the steering wheel!

Electricity did not arrive in Kentmere until 1963, indicative of this peaceful valley where little changes.

*Strictly speaking a town rather than
a village, Keswick plays host to a large number of visitors throughout the year.
It has a superb position, backed by Skiddaw and overlooking Derwent Water
and the surrounding fells*

Although Keswick is generally thronged with people, it remains a pleasant town to visit, and somehow manages to convey a holiday atmosphere. Pedestrianisation of the centre around the Moot Hall has done the town a great favour. However, the large number of outdoor leisure shops is arguably at the expense of a wider range of other shops. There is an excellent lively Saturday market.

The Moot Hall, in the centre, houses an information centre and occasional exhibitions. Other exhibitions can be seen at the pleasantly traditional Keswick Museum at Fitz Park. Plays and other cultural events are staged by the Theatre by the Lake, a superb asset to the town.

In 2001 the cricket ground in Fitz Park, with its splendid backdrop of Skiddaw, won the Wisden accolade of "the most beautiful ground in Britain".

A flat but popular circular walk of seven miles runs along the Old Railway that follows the River Greta from the north side of Keswick to Threlkeld.

Keswick's parish church of St Kentigern (one of the town's several churches) is at Crosthwaite, on the western edge of the town (below). Canon Rawnsley, the founder of the National Trust, was vicar here for 34 years, and the baptistry is a memorial to him. Also interesting is the white marble memorial to Southey with an epitaph by Wordsworth.

LAKESIDE *above*

A mile north of Newby Bridge, this popular spot on Lake Windermere is busy with steam trains and boats coming and going

Looking down from the slopes of Gummers Howe (above) the station platform and landing stages at Lakeside can be seen above the mass of hawthorn blossom. Steam trains ply the scenic little line which follows the River Leven for three and a half miles from Haverthwaite. A popular way of extending the trip is then to board one of the boats run by Windermere Lake Cruises (right). Alternatively in summer a little ferry crosses the lake to Fellfoot park and garden (owned by the National Trust). This is a good place for a picnic, a visit to the tea-room, or a wander around the Victorian gardens and along the lakeshore enjoying the lovely views.

The Aquatarium at Lakeside is a popular visitor choice, where you can be nose to nose with the fish then walk in a tunnel beneath them. One of the displays charts the voyage of a Lake District river from its head to Morecambe Bay.

LORTON *right*

Situated in the lushly pastoral Vale of Lorton, four miles from Cockermouth, the village is split into two settlements, High and Low Lorton. Neither settlement has an obvious village centre but both are attractive places in which to wander. The Wheatsheaf pub and a little shop are the only tourist facilities

In High Lorton, a yew tree that was the subject of a Wordsworth poem can be seen growing near the original Jennings Brewery building. Jennings, a successful regional brewery, was founded in 1828 and later moved to its present site in Cockermouth. The old brewery has now become the village hall.

The village encompasses two private estates, no doubt encouraged by the rich meadowlands, and the unusual battlemented circular smokehouse at Lorton Park can be seen from the road. Low Lorton lies by the River Cocker. Water from the river and the fast-flowing streams in the village was used to power flour and linen mills.

LOWTHER *right*

Lowther Castle is situated five miles south of Penrith in beautiful parkland on the eastern fringes of the Lake District. The estate villages of Lowther New Town and Lowther Village lie about half a mile from the castle and church

A footpath leads past the front gateway of the spectacular Gothic ruin of the castle but the site is strictly out of bounds, because of the ever-present danger of falling masonry.

The castle was built in about 1810 and designed by Robert Smirke for the Lowther family, very influential local landowners who lived at nearby Askham Hall. The architect was then only 25 years old and this was his first commission. The "Yellow Earl", the fifth Lord Lonsdale (1880-1944) was a great character but notoriously extravagant. The castle had over 60 indoor staff, frequently seeing to the needs of visiting royalty and the Kaiser (the German emperor), as well as 30 or more gardeners. However, the extravagances eventually nearly broke the family and, by the 1950s, the castle was in such disrepair that it was partially demolished and became the romantic ruin that can be seen today.

NEAR SAWREY *above*

Near and Far Sawrey lie a mile apart between Lake Windermere and Esthwaite Water in a lovely pastoral setting that is resonant of Beatrix Potter's watercolours

Hill Top, Beatrix Potter's house, is situated in Near Sawrey, making this the better known of the two villages. The house (below) now owned by the National Trust is open to the public on certain days. The author's furniture, china and watercolours are on display. In the kitchen garden there are delightful little tableaux which are reminiscent of scenes from *Peter Rabbit*.

Esthwaite Water, which is very close to Near Sawrey, is gently pretty and is a popular lake for fishermen.

Far Sawrey, the village closer to Windermere and accessible on foot from the ferry, has very little car parking. The handsome Sawrey Hotel lies near to a footpath leading up to Claife Heights. The beautifully situated St Peter's Church lies across the fields from the village. This large church was originally built to accommodate 400 people since many of the large houses in the area had a number of servants. The building is mainly of local slate rubble with sandstone dressing.

NETHER WASDALE

*Nether Wasdale is the tiniest of
settlements, no more than a hamlet,
and lies between Gosforth, Santon
Bridge and Wastwater. Its attraction
lies in its wonderfully skewed ratio
of buildings; the one church and two
pubs nearly outnumber all
other buildings*

Nether Wasdale (right), sometimes
known as Strands, is picturesquely
situated at the foot of a hill, with a view
of Wastwater Screes in the distance. It
makes a wonderful place to stop and
recuperate after a hard day's walking in
Wasdale.

The little white church, dedicated to
St Michael and All Angels, was originally
a chapel of ease for St Bees Priory. It
contains remains of early murals and
some beautifully carved oak furnishings.

The village really comes alive on the
first Saturday in May with maypole
dancing, a children's fancy dress parade,
clog dancing, plenty of beer and a brass
band.

POOLEY BRIDGE *below*

The village lies close to the northern tip of Ullswater where the River Eamont leaves the lake, about five miles south-west of Penrith

Until recently Pooley Bridge seemed to be a quiet backwater; now it bustles with visitors and sometimes feels as if it is in danger of being swamped. The narrowness of the old bridge (right), built for horses and carts, causes elaborate manoeuvres as cars try to cross. The Ullswater Steamer Company boat links here with Howtown and Glenridding and connects with excellent walks to the east of the lake. There are also walks from Pooley Bridge up onto Moordivock, an area rich in prehistoric remains, including The Cockpit stone circle.

PATTERDALE *left*

On the road between Kirkstone Pass and Ullswater, the Patterdale valley is an important centre for mountain walkers

Towering above the small centre of Patterdale is the Helvellyn mountain range. One of the most popular routes to the summit lies along the skyline. The Coast to Coast long-distance footpath passes through the village, and many walkers use the excellent youth hostel.

The name "Patterdale" comes from a visit by Saint Patrick in the 5th century. He landed on the Duddon Sands and travelled to Ullswater, where he preached and baptised local people.

Across the Goldrill Beck lie the idyllic cottages of Rooking. One of these (above) is named "Wordsworth's Cottage". The story goes that he came close to owning it. How the peaceful character of the hamlet might have been altered had he done so!

RAVENGLASS *above & left*

The boundary of the Lake District National Park includes a short section of coastline, an indication of the scenic and environmental importance of Ravenglass and its surrounding estuary. The village is situated at a point on the estuary where the Irt, the Mite and the Esk rivers converge

Ravenglass was originally a Roman supply port and there are significant remains of the old bath-house still standing. A Roman road led from the port through Eskdale, over Hardknott Pass guarded by Hardknott Fort and on to Ambleside. Today this characterful little village, with its cheerful front gardens, makes for a worthwhile trip in its own right as well as being the terminal for the "La'al Ratty" narrow gauge railway. Ravenglass is also close to the impressive gardens and house at Muncaster.

ROSTHWAITE *above & right*

This unspoiled little village is in the Borrowdale valley, on the road from Derwent Water to Honister Pass. Rosthwaite still has working farms and the herds of Herdwick sheep and drystone walls make this an archetypal Lakeland village

Rosthwaite is a popular starting point for many walks, including the one up to Watendlath. There is very little parking in the village but the excellent bus service up the valley from Keswick is a useful alternative to driving. The village has a hotel, a little shop and a café called "The Flock Inn" at Yew Tree Farm which stands in a delightfully rural environment.

The Borrowdale Show in mid September is held in fields adjacent to the village. It is a wonderful opportunity to watch all the traditional sports, such as fell racing, Cumberland and Westmorland wrestling, terrier racing and tug-of-war.

The village lies just off the main road from Ambleside to Grasmere. Rydal Mount, one of several characterful houses, is best known for being Wordsworth's home for the last four decades of his life

In contrast to the simplicity of Dove Cottage, Rydal Mount (right) was quite grand and spacious. It is now open to the public and contains fine furniture from Wordsworth's era together with manuscripts, family possessions and portraits. The gardens are laid out as they were when the poet was in residence. In spring the ground adjacent to Rydal church – known as "Dora's Field" – is carpeted with wild daffodils, originally planted in memory of Wordsworth's favourite daughter after she died in 1847.

Opposite Rydal Mount is Rydal Hall (bottom), an imposing 17th-century house now owned by the Diocese of Carlisle and used as a conference and retreat centre. The formal gardens are open to the public with a little café nearby. The Rydal Beck cascades down a rock ravine. The noise of rushing water can be heard from the formal gardens.

Seatoller & Stonethwaite

The two tiny villages lie close to each other on the valley floor of Borrowdale. Just to the west of them the road climbs sharply up the one-in-four gradient of the Honister Pass

Stonethwaite (below) is in the only side valley which breaches the great eastern wall of fells in Borrowdale. Wainwright's Coast to Coast route links the two villages. Both villages have welcoming spots to stop for a break and, if necessary, to shelter from the often inclement Lakeland weather.

Seatoller (right) is little more than a cluster of houses around a farm but it has an excellent information centre in a converted barn.

Borrowdale Church, which is near the road junction leading to Stonethwaite, is a simple roughcast building with some interesting windows and a churchyard which includes the grave of Bob Graham, the famous fell-runner who, in the 1930s, established a record for running to the top of 42 Lake District peaks (the "Bob Graham Round") in less than 24 hours.

TROUTBECK *left*

Troutbeck stretches out for more than a mile along a side road off the Kirkstone Pass main road that links Windermere and Ullswater. It contains many wonderful examples of the Lake District's most attractive architecture

Troutbeck has very little by way of a village centre, although it has two pubs and a village shop. The only way to fully appreciate the many lovely buildings is on foot. Townend House (owned by the National Trust) is at the southern end of the village. Built in 1626, it is a remarkably intact example of a yeoman's house. The large round chimney stacks are typical of more well-to-do houses of the period but it is questionable whether their design was practical or mere ostentation. Opposite Town End there is a handsome bank barn, one of many in the village. These took practical advantage of the steeply sloping terrain.

The church, unusually just called "Jesus Church", has a Burne-Jones window, and a churchyard filled with a cheery mass of daffodils in spring.

ST BEES *right & left*

Not strictly in the Lake District but a popular place to visit on the coast, four miles south of Whitehaven

St Bees not only has one of the rare golden sandy beaches in Cumbria, but also the magnificent four-mile long sandstone St Bees Head (left) which is a nature reserve. The Coast to Coast walk starts here, and climbs up and over the South Head, dropping to Fleswick Bay before rising again over the North Head and the lighthouse. In early summer the headlands are decked with wildflowers, and the cliffs are noisy with the hubbub of nesting seabirds. An occasional puffin can be spotted, and on a clear day the distant views to the Isle of Man are excellent.

The village proper is set back a little from the coast. The priory church of St Bega is renowned for its richly decorated Norman doorway. The priory (above) was established by Bega, an Irish nun who was shipwrecked here in the 9th century. Close to the church is St Bees School, founded in 1583. The original redstone quadrangle bears the coat of arms of its founder, Edmund Grindal, Archbishop of Canterbury in the reign of Elizabeth I.

WASDALE HEAD *above*

More of a hamlet than a true village, this is the only clutch of buildings for many miles around. It has a magnificent setting just north-east of Wastwater in an arena of dramatic mountains which include Scafell

The historic Wasdale Head Inn provides a useful stop at the end of a day's walking and has home-brewed beers which are made using spring water from Yewbarrow.

The tiny St Olaf's Church is almost hidden behind its screen of ancient yews. Some of the gravestones commemorate climbers who died in the surrounding mountains. Inside, the impressive roof beams are thought to have come from Viking ships. A delightful leaded window is engraved with the inscription: "I will lift up mine eyes unto the hills from whence cometh my strength" – a First World War memorial to members of the Fell and Rock Climbing Club.

The Wasdale Show in early October features Herdwick sheep and a great variety of traditional sporting events take place, including hound-trailing.

WATENDLATH *below & right*

Situated at the end of an extremely narrow and twisting road from Derwent Water, the little hamlet is better approached on foot, either from Rosthwaite or Ashness – a route which also gives you the chance of visiting the Lodore Falls on the way

Watendlath is the sort of place where ducks and geese seem to have an equal right to the road as cars. A working farm often means that sheep-shearing, dipping and gathering take place under the nose of visitors. An ancient packhorse bridge (left) crosses Watendlath Beck soon after it leaves the tarn. Otherwise the hamlet principally consists of a farmhouse or two, one selling teas and another hiring out rowing boats for trout fishing. The entire area is in the ownership of the National Trust.

The writer Hugh Walpole used the remote position of Watendlath as a setting for *Judith Paris*, one of four novels in his Cumberland family saga, and a house sporting a slate sign claims to be the home of this fictional heroine.

WINDERMERE *left & above*

The only town in the Lake District accessible by rail, Windermere is the terminus of a branch line from Oxenholme Station, Kendal. An excellent bus service connects it to Ambleside and Keswick. Alternatively Windermere is eight miles by road from Kendal

Many visitors catch their first view of the Lake District as they drive over the crest above Windermere. The town is not as immediately attractive as many other places in the Lake District but for visitors without a car it could certainly be a handy base. Along with the adjoining village of Bowness, it has a good range of accommodation plus pubs, cafés and restaurants.

Various short walks from the town go to spectacular viewpoints including Biskey Howe, Brant Fell, School Knott and Orrest Head. A path from St Mary's Church leads down to Queen Adelaide's Hill and on to the steamboat museum.

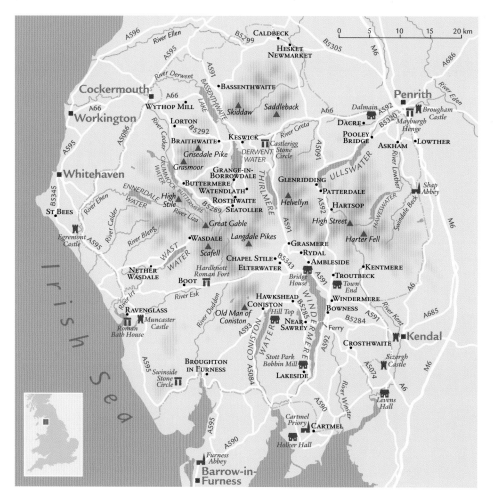

First published in 2009 by Myriad Books Limited
35 Bishopsthorpe Road, London SE26 4PA

Photographs copyright © Val Corbett
Text copyright © Val Corbett

Val Corbett has asserted her right under the Copyright, Designs and Patents Act 1998 to be identified as the author of this work.

All rights reserved. No part of this publication may be reproduced, stored in a retrieval system, or transmitted in any form or by any means, electronic, mechanical, photocopying, recording or otherwise, without the prior permission of the copyright owners.

ISBN 1 84746 265 0
EAN 978 1 84746 265 7

Designed by Jerry Goldie Graphic Design

Map by Stephen Dew

Printed in China

www.myriadbooks.com

Front cover: Braithwaite;
back cover: Buttermere;
title page: Cartmel

Key
- ▲ Peaks
- 🏰 Castle
- Ancient Site
- Historic Building
- Abbey
- National Park boundary